LIFE
After

How to Pick Up the Pieces
After Brokenness

Geneva Cummins

Life After: How to Pick Up the Pieces After Brokenness

Library of Congress Cataloging-In-Publication Data:

An application to register this book for cataloging has been submitted to the Library of Congress.

Cummins, Geneva

Unless otherwise noted, all Scripture are taken from the King James Version. Public domain.

ISBN: 978-1-5136-5442-3

Photography by Kimberly Taylor

Cover and interior design by Stacey Grainger

Printed in the United States of America

First Edition

To every woman who has tried, failed,
and triumphed in life, love, and laughter.

To Linda Clemons and Sisterpreneurs...

Without you, none of this would have been possible. You opened your world of entrepreneurs and tribes (as you call them), and they showed me how to become a success in many areas of life. The women I have met through Sisterpreneurs are now my own sisters. We take up the charge to blaze a mark of significance in the world.

Thank you for mentoring me, and most of all, for being my friend.

Thank you Yolanda Billings

CONTENTS

FOREWORD

I was a "30 something" mother of four in a delight-
fully happy marriage when life took a left turn, as
it often does, and ended up nowhere near the des-
tination I had intended. A happy family, financial
comfort and sincere dedication to a religion are not
guarantee that things will always go your way. And
they didn't.

My husband of nearly twenty years, at the time, was
caught up in a legal battle that took on a life of its
own. He ended up to my utter amazement, in prison
for fourteen months and one week. To say I was
shocked would be an utter understatement.

But go he did and I was left at home, for those ardu-
ous months, a single mother who was married. I was
a working mom who was also a stay at home mom. I

was the head of our congregation's women's organization and simultaneously was in great need of being ministered to. Body, mind and soul.

My experiences are, thankfully, unique. But more important than that is that each of us finds ourselves at one point or another, given enough years, having life take a left turn on us. We become disoriented, at times angry and definitely feeling a depth of loneliness that is breathtaking.

And from our most desperate times come our most glorious lessons, blessings and insights. These dreadful moments turn us back to our faith and to humanity and when we allow them to, they grow us, make us stronger and call us into service of others.

What felt like the end of my joy was the beginning of my best adventures. I am a better wife, mother, and human. What I believed to be our family's embarrassment turned into keynote speeches and new career opportunities.

I am an Executive Coach not in spite of having a husband who is a felon, but because our journey through that train wreck made us better than we could have been without it.

My "Life After" is where I met and coached Geneva Cummins. We are connected on a soul level because when things go wrong so many more things can go so right. We instantly connected as souls and sisters who have suffered the pains and emerged into the sunshine of relief. Through my time working with Geneva, I was humbled to know with a soul with such great depth, kindness and wisdom.

Geneva's life experience, faith and deep desire to love and serve others has created in her a Rare Gem. She is a diamond that sparkles even without the sunshine because her light comes from within.

I have had the honor of sharing my life's work with Geneva and in so doing, have been exposed to a beautiful soul with so much to teach us all.

As I sit in my office writing about my friend, I imagine you, the reader, sitting on a bus, a plane or having a lunch break read in your car. I see you turning the pages and tucking in to a book that's time has come. I couldn't be more delighted for us all.

Michelle Young
MichelleAtPlay.com

INTRODUCTION

Life Happens

In 1974, The Average White Band released a hit song titled *Pick Up the Pieces*. According to one artist in the Scotsmen group, the instrumental song was written as a response to failure they had experienced in the music industry. Apparently, the band had spent a lot of time making no money, so they felt it appropriate to release a tune that was primarily instrumental with an occasional shout. The group's producer was hesitant to release the song on the second album, in fear that no one would want to listen to the funky jazz sounds of Scotsmen without lyrics. In part, the producer was right. When first released in the United Kingdom (July 1974), the song failed

"Life can only
be understood
backwards;
but it must be
lived forwards."

Soren Kierkegaard,
Theologian

to make the charts. Shortly after, *Pick Up the Pieces* was released in the United States (October 1974). To their surprise, the single rose to the fifth spot on the soul charts. And if that wasn't enough, *Pick Up the Pieces* was recognized by the *Billboard* as the number 20 song in 1975. Wow! A far cry from utter failure just one year prior. Much like the experiences of the Average White Band, each of encounters struggles and triumphs.

Life is Like a Puzzle

There are countless events, or pieces that come into play during your life's journey. Think of each event as a puzzle, a tapestry of art that is unfinished. When you purchase a puzzle, there are dozens of pieces in the box that you must arrange to form the picture depicted on the cover. From this perspective, the idea of picking up the pieces does not necessarily mean something was broken to begin with. None-the-less, the pieces are shuffled, and you have the task to make meaning of the parts. You didn't make it that way; you did not choose the shapes of each piece or decide how many pieces it would take to form the picture. What counts is your desire to pick up the pieces and turn it into something beautiful.

Most of us don't look at life this way, as something that's within our power to mold. Instead we feel as if we're on the defensive—life happened, now what am I going to do? How am I going to get through this situation or fix that problem? We tend to react with panic, anxiety, stress, or other negative responses. We start to pick up the pieces as we move through life, but there is more to creating a work of art than throwing things together haphazardly. If we don't take time to fit the pieces together properly, instead of forcing mismatches together in desperation, we may finish the puzzle, but the picture will be warped. It won't reflect the full potential of what it was created to be. In the real sense of who we were designed to be, this is no way to live our lives—scrambling and throwing things back together any kind of way? No way, not at all. The missing piece is to live with intention. We must ask ourselves several questions:

- Why am I putting these pieces together?
- What is my deepest motive?
- What is the ultimate image I wish to create?

As we work through our puzzles in life, it's often tempting to look outward at what others are arranging with their own pieces. We must keep in mind not to take broken pieces from other puzzles to try to complete our own. In this case, we might end up with a similar picture, but a false and distorted image that's not our own. It takes time to pick up the pieces, and rightfully so. As each day passes, we add and subtract pieces. Some are small and delight, while others are large and impressed with curves and sharper edges. Embrace every moment, every step of life and watch the canvas bloom. You might not see the scene coming together right away but trust the process to take form and move forward as intended by the God.

Even in the darkest of times, eventually light peers in radiance. While one puzzle is completed, another is created. Infinity is the essence of evolution. From this perspective, we can truly understand that there is always *Life After!*

This book's message is universal. So many of us get stuck in life's journey and fail to realize that the journey itself is full of *Life After*. Life happens to each of us, from the time we're born until the time we die. There is a mixture of good and not so good moments. You will experience the ups and downs, both overwhelming and exciting. There will be times when the pain of life hits you so hard you will forget to breathe—unthinkable moments like the death of a child. Then there will be times when the pain of life takes your breath away in joy, like during the birth of a child. No matter the emotion, there is *Life After.* This is a magical journey.

My Own Life After

At 17 years old, I was just graduating from high school and had been accepted into John Jay College. There was a clear idea of the path I was going to take and how my life would unfold. Then the unimaginable. I found out I was pregnant. I thought the world was going to end at that very second.

I was young and being raised with five siblings. How in the world was I going to tell my mom? I could not see beyond that moment, so how could there possibly be a *Life After*? It was an overwhelming time and I had no idea how to handle it. My mom, Queen Esther as she's called, told me, "You're not the first person to get pregnant and you won't be the last." She was assuring me in her own way that things were going to be okay. I still didn't see it yet. All I thought was, this was not how I planned my life and now it is over. I wanted to be a college student without a care in the world, doing all the things I assumed college students do hanging out, traveling, trying new things, and just having a good time. Having a baby seemed to make those things impossible.

When I reflect on the birth of my son, Curtis, it was a scary time and I wondered how I was going to make it. Making bottles, changing diapers, and having people tell you how disappointed they were in you was extremely difficult; not having the needed support from his father did not help matters either. It was not easy. Considering I was going to college full time and working part time, I had very little time for a social life. The experience of being a young single mother was hard, but I do not regret it. My mom did not believe in abortions and I am so glad that she didn't, because in that case that little boy may not be here. I thank God that I had him, even though it was a piece of my puzzle that I had to wait a long time before seeing its beauty. Curtis has always been a great son and is now a grown man. He has a beautiful wife named Amena and my precious grandson, Chase. I did not know it at the time, but generations of love and joy would come from picking up the pieces as a teenage mom.

I later married a wonderful man named Winston, and we had a beautiful baby girl, Karess. This experience was different. I say different, not better, because each experience in your life is valuable in its own way and teaches you something new. With Curtis, I was single and a teenager; with Karess, I was married and more mature. Both experiences with my children have been wonderful and have made me a better person. When I got married, I was starting another puzzle with a whole new set of pieces to pick up along with Winston, Karess, and Curtis, who was now eleven years old. While we grew as a family, we had to make the puzzle fit together.

There will be people in your life that you will want to take with you as you start on a new puzzle. You will shift, bend, and nearly break trying to add in their piece to your puzzle, and then have to pry them out later when you realize they just don't take on the right form to fit *this puzzle*. This may not be the season of your life for them. On the other hand, there are moments when you align with someone and you find your pieces fall together beautifully. Winston becoming the father of Curtis was an example of the pieces coming together. He looked at the cover of this new puzzle box and saw his family and began to make the pieces fit together. He didn't see Curtis as another man's child; he saw him and said, "That's my son." The puzzle pieces took their shape.

Sometimes we try new pieces that simply don't work. They may seem like a good fit at first glance, but in the end, it was just an illusion. We must wait until the right pieces of the puzzle come together for us, and sometimes waiting is hard. I've learned that if you don't be patient, you can lose your family, your home, and everything that's important because you're searching for something that is not part of the puzzle that was created for you. This can cause your puzzle to be incomplete. Even so, there are times when that puzzle is never completed; the good news is that those leftover pieces can be recycled and redesigned into something new, and that starts your *Life After*.

You Are Not Alone in Your Journey

In September of 2014 I had an operation on my esophagus. I was diagnosed with Barrett's esophagus, which is a condition when the lining of the esophagus starts to corrode and can evolve into cancer. I had been suffering from acid reflux for five years. Prior to the operation, I could not lie down without three or four pillows at time. Sometimes I would wake from my sleep throwing up my food which I had eaten 7 hours earlier, because I had not digested it. This was very painful. I was being treated with different types of medicines, but nothing helped. I spent many nights in so much pain, crying by myself in my own private agony. Have you ever been in a place where you get tired of saying what's wrong with you because you think people are tired of hearing it or they really don't understand? You become so entangled in that moment that you close the door to what's next. I know what it feels like when the pain of a situation is unbearable, and you want to die. Maybe not literally—you just want the pain to go away. Those days when you can't get up or you don't want to get up; those moments when the sun is shining outside but not in you. When you see yourself going to work, walking around, and entertaining people, as if this is all a movie starring you but you're watching from the outside. You're talking, but it feels like someone else is. I walked around like that for months. Yes, months, I thank God that one day the right doctor heard my cry and changed my situation around. I had the operation and now I don't throw up anymore, and I can sleep with or without a pillow. I can eat without worrying about whether my food will come up later. I can go on vacation and enjoy myself, and best of all, I'm not crying anymore. I kept going and walked right into another *Life After* moment.

While we all fall into dark moments, this is also for those whose joy of an experience can cause them to miss *Life After* moments. I've known friends who lived in a season where everything was perfect, but when things started going downhill, they could not see it. All they talked about was that era in their lives when they were on top of the world. We can get stuck even in happy moments because we don't want to let it go of what was. When this happens, we end up living our life stuck in the frame of one puzzle and never allow ourselves to see the other puzzles that await us.

Each of us has our own *Life After* story. This book was written to let you know that you are not alone. Everyone does not have a circle of family or loved ones to get them through life's struggles, or even to rejoice with them during moments of triumph. I want this book to be your anchor. If you find yourself in a dark place during this journey called life and you can't see your way out, read one of these stories in these pages. Hopefully something that is said will resonate with you, even though your situation may be completely different. Take time to engage with the reflection questions at the end of each section. There is power and personal growth in introspection. My greatest desire is for you to hold on to hope and experience the sparkle of *Life After*.

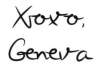

Xoxo,
Geneva

"Don't be afraid
of your fears."

Anonymous

Life After

CHAPTER TWO

It's All Good

Lana's Story...

I didn't want to accept it. I didn't want to claim it. I just didn't want to acknowledge it. After experiencing awful pain in my shoulder for weeks, I was diagnosed with lupus.

During my first visit to the doctor's, I was misdiagnosed with bursitis. The pain wouldn't go away, despite the strong medication. My doctor was an amazing advocate. Instead of simply increasing my medication, or totally dismissing me, she decided to run additional tests. The results showed I had lupus. All I knew about lupus was that a friend's cousin suffered from it and didn't survive. I was consumed by thoughts of fear and death, and immediately went on the defensive. The doctor filled in some gaps and informed me that lupus is a systemic autoimmune disease that occurs when your body's immune system attacks your own tissues and organs. The resulting inflammation can affect your joints, skin, kidneys, blood cells, brain, heart and lungs. No matter the explanation, I refused to accept the diagnosis.

After the initial findings, I was sent to see a specialist and undergo another series of tests. The specialist was not at all like my primary care physician. This woman was stern, quite stoned-hearted, and had no bedside manners. I can still hear the robotic intonation in her voice, "You absolutely have lupus and you need to take this medication. If you become pregnant, you cannot have the child because it will be born with many challenges and disorders." At that time, I had a young son who always wanted siblings, and I knew I wanted more kids. My body went somewhat numb. For her to basically tell me I had to be okay with aborting my future child—I was not okay with that. I decided to do my own research to find another specialist. I owed it to myself to get a second opinion and broaden my options moving forward.

The specialist I chose on my own had the perseverance I was looking for. She looked at the results and was optimistic from the onset. Her response was, "Yes, you have lupus but it's not the end of the world." I didn't quite know what that meant so I continued to panic, *Am I going to die like the other woman I had known?* The doctor assured me, "Absolutely not. We're more advanced now. We have different ways to stay on top of it. It's going to take a while to get you stabilized and back to normal, but we will." Her encouragement made me feel a little bit better. However, I was still in denial and very hesitant about taking the medication. I avoided it completely.

In the months that followed, I fell into a rut. I saw the pieces strewn before me but lacked the will to begin picking them up. Every morning I struggled to get moving, dress myself, and do the things with my son that I was accustomed to doing. It took some time, but one day I woke up and snapped out of it. I told myself, *"You've got to do this for your child, you've got to get it together, and you're going to survive."* That was the moment I chose to live and pick up the first piece. I took my medication, went to my appointments, and followed a plan with my doctor. After about twelve weeks, I noticed my energy levels slowly increasing. I no longer had to tell my son, "No, mom's too tired today." I pushed forward with the treatment plan and the support of family, friends, and prayer.

As time passed and things started to pick up, I began dating again and met someone. Five years after my diagnosis, God blessed me with the pregnancy of my second child. I remember the doctor saying, "You're high risk. Not only are you over a certain age, but you have lupus as well. The good news is your lupus is fairly stable, so we just have to watch you." This was a blessing. I made sure to listen to the doctor's advice and take my time. Despite my efforts, that pregnancy ended in a miscarriage. To-say-the-least, I was completely devastated. Why me? Why did this happen? I began to fall into another bout of depression. It was hard, but I had to remind myself not to go back to that dark place I was in before. I had to push forward to what God had in store for me. I continued to think, *"No one can take this dream away from me."*

Two months after miscarrying, I got pregnant again. I was even more careful this time around, and I had the most amazing doctors who were with me every step of the way. I was fortunate enough to give birth to a healthy baby girl who will be five years old this year. Given the odds that were stacked against me, I was overwhelmed and grateful. What happened next was further miraculous and left me floored—I no longer showed traces of lupus in my body. This is rare. It very rarely happens that a patient has a strong case of lupus, then ends up with no signs at all. It was truly amazing!

I knew this victory was due to my faith in God, continuous prayers from friends and family, and my refusal to fully concede to the diagnosis. A big part of the battle was choosing to live and having a reason to push forward. Instead of giving in to my diagnosis, I vowed to live for my son and any children to come after him. Surrounding myself with people that supported and encouraged me when I felt like giving up also turned the tide. If we can find a way to stay positive and avoid negativity in our inner circle, it can make all the difference in the world.

From the tenacity to battle through my diagnosis and encircled by loved ones, I was able to pick up the pieces and enjoy the beauty of my *Life After*.

PICK UP THE PIECES...

- When you have a high-value goal, recognize your limits, but push forward anyway.
- Consistency is the antidote to failure
- Identify your "We won't quit" tribe

What are you hoping, wishing, believing for?

> *Jesus looked at them and said, "With man this is impossible, but with God all things are possible.*
>
> **(Matthew 19:26)**

Why is it important that you remain steadfast in your belief?

> *Be strong and take heart, and have no fear of them:*
> *For it is the Lord your God who is going with you;*
> *He will not take away his help from you.*

(Deuteronomy 31:6)

CHAPTER THREE

Take the Leap

Sylvia's Story...

Given the decades of my life spent in that community, there was no doubt it was a place of security and comfort. I was part of that church ministry for 22 years. With the sudden passing of the founding pastor, a transition took shape in my church life. You often hear people saying they left church because of church hurt. I left my church because I did not like

"Faith is taking
the first step
even when you
can't see the
whole staircase."

Dr. Marin Luther King

the direction the church was going under the new leadership. So after much prayer I made the decision to leave.

Over the years, I wore many hats in my church's community—I was the audio technician working in the sound booth almost every regular services; twice on Sundays, Wednesdays and Friday's and all the scheduled and unscheduled services during the week and throughout the month. In addition I was a lead member of the women's department, the Bible School and helped with several other services and clinics held at the church. Initially all members were asked to attend at least three services a week. In truth, more evenings of the week were spent in the church than at home. I loved the guidance from my pastor and the fellowship from other members of the congregation.

I had completed graduate work a short time prior and excited to introduce new ideas. However, I often felt my voice wasn't heard. Whether it was a matter of conflicting opinions or bad timing, the bottom line was I never saw my ideas implemented or my talents fully used on a more practical end. It was an incredibly difficult time leading up to the decision, but I would soon come to realize that leaving was the easy part.

I had questioned my place in that church for three long years after the founder's passing, and I finally realized I had to make a change. It was time to leave. I spoke with my pastor, provided training on all the roles I held, and in a spirit of love and understanding, I broke away from the ministry. When I left the ministry, never would I have imagined that the friendships that was made over the years would end; no more calls, text, or an email.

This began my search for another place to call home. Since my Sunday mornings were dedicated to ministering as a chaplain at a local hospital, I typically had to rush from the hospital to church without a moment to breathe in between. Every week felt like a race— my time was simply stretched thin. For the next four years I drifted from church to church. This was a lonely time in the wilderness, aiming to find the right fit. I vowed to keep an open mind but could not seem to get it together. Soon doubt crept into my thoughts— *was I constantly comparing to my former church? What was I really looking for?* The time I spent in limbo came to a head one evening in April. My former pastor called and asked if we could meet. Soon after, we were sitting together in his office. In our catching up, I let him know that I was still looking for a new ministry to call home. He invited me to reconnect with the church. Even if I were to ignore some of the factors of my original choice, the conflict with Sunday morning duties at the hospital ministry reinforced my stance of not returning. The pastor understood and wished me well and asked that I at least visit soon. I mentioned I'd try to come by sometime and he implored, "No, really, please come back to visit."

It just so happened the week was leading up to Good Friday, and the guest speaker slated to attend was someone I admire and followed online. It seemed like the perfect opportunity to visit, so I kept my promise. The service was truly awesome. I connected with scores of friends I hadn't seen in many years. One woman had also left the ministry years ago, and we embraced over that shared struggle. Amid our conversation she enlightened me with a pivotal piece of advice. She suggested in my search, I write out the main things I wanted to find in a ministry and those I wanted to avoid. She stressed, "Include any pet peeves you may have about a church." I essentially needed to put the vision into words and watch it come to pass. That's exactly what I did.

Two weeks later, one of my coworkers suggested a church location I might find interesting. As she noted, the congregation size was like the one I had in mind, there was a great community, and best of all, the first service on Sunday started at two o'clock. It sounded like the perfect match! It wasn't long after that I chose to become a member of this ministry. All the gifts that were lying dormant at the other ministry were suddenly brought to light and amplified. This church services start in the afternoon, which afforded me the opportunity to continue the ministry in the hospital. I found a balance that allowed me to strengthen my bond with the church and God. The bonus was that I still had time to focus on my marriage and other relationships. I forged new friendships and prospered in fellowship with the congregation. I finally found my *Life After*.

For anyone going through a transition to leave a place of comfort, whether it be a steady job, long-term relationships, or trusted community— don't despair. While the risk of a new environment may seem daunting, your actions will pay off. Be intentional. Know what you seek and what to avoid. Envision your goal, pick up the pieces, and take the leap into your *Life After*.

PICK UP THE PIECES...

- Pretend like, act like, you are not afraid
- Disempower the disappointments of life
- Harness the power of possibility

I am afraid to do _____
_____, but I am going to do it afraid.

*For God hath not given us the spirit of fear;
but of power, and of love, and of a sound mind.*"

(2 Timothy 1:7)

Think about a past tough decision you made. What was the results of your actions?

Your word is a lamp to guide me
and a light for my path.

(Psalm 119:105)

You can spend minutes, hours, days, weeks or months over-analyzing a situation; trying to put the pieces together, justifying what could've, would've happened ... or you can just leave the pieces on the floor and move on"

Tupac Shakur

CHAPTER FOUR

You Can Move On

Carolyn's Story...

If you follow the rules, everything works out. At least that's what I grew up believing. I went through life dutifully in every sense of the word. I graduated from college, became a teacher, married my husband, and built a beautiful home with two children. Everything was perfect, everything was fine. I had just started my own dance school and was getting ready for an upcoming recital. Until *life happened*. Almost with the snap of a finger, my life took a turn for the worst.

One morning I woke to find my husband had a stroke. While dealing with my husband in the hospital just like that I was faced with eviction from our current residence, as we waited for the new house under contract to be built which now had to stop because he was the primary financial provider for the family. I was in a limbo, to say it mildly. In an instance, I went from marching faithfully to finding my husband nearly dead, the marshal at my door, my belongings on the street, and two young boys to raise alone. I was absolutely crushed.

I will never forget that day when the marshal came to my door, the neighbors tried to help, "Give her a chance to get her things together. Her husband is on his deathbed." He didn't care. The fake landlord who was the landlord's nephew had power or attorney from the real landlord who was a personal friend "with dementia". He threw me out immediately putting everything I owned on the street because he wanted the house for a friend. I left that chaos to go to the hospital to take my husband off life support.

Life After

My children didn't understand why the life support had to be pulled from their dad. They were overhearing conversations no child should have to hear. The following day, he went on to glory. It was all too much to bear. And, to add insult to pain, I didn't have a place for family and friends to pay their last respects to my boys and I as a family in mourning.

In the midst of a storm God does make a way. Using funds from the first ticket purchases of a dance recital I was sponsoring; I was able to put a down payment on a place to temporarily live. After the funeral, I wanted nothing more than to rest and mourn my husband, but life doesn't wait for you. I was on the clock with two months to prepare for the dance recital. Even though I was receiving condolences, the recital had to go on for guests who purchased tickets.

Between the impending recital, the upcoming move, and the crushing stress of low funds, I had to be a rock for my children. There were times when I wanted to die. I didn't think, in my wildest dreams, I would ever be able to survive and get through that dark place.

In those moments I reflected on lessons from my mother. She always said, *no matter what is going on with your life, you lift yourself off the ground, hold your head high, and never give up in the power of prayer.* My mom did not give me this advice to demean the struggles; depression is real. Problems and obstacles are real. Nevertheless, we must pray, and persevere.

For me, the students were a focal point in my ability to push through. I worked with kids and would listen to the stories of what they were going through. When they laid their burdens on me, I was the one to encourage them to keep moving just as my mother did for me. This was especially true for my own kids who no longer had a father. I became the pillar of support that my students and children looked to for comfort. When you become the rock, you dig deeper within yourself to find strength to pick up the pieces for yourself and those around you.

Later in life, the pain I held in my heart healed and I met a wonderful man who I'm still with today. It took time, but I was slowly able to let him into my heart.

He helped me to raise my children and supported me as I grew my business. I was able to keep the dance studio operating and I picked up the pieces one by one. My husband came from a prior marriage and had children of his own. With time and intention, we were able to create a *Life After* together, forming an intertwined puzzle between our families. Life has seemingly come together as we celebrated the 90th birthday for my mother. Seeing everyone together, enjoying the company of one another was a long time in the making. I am grateful for the support of family and friends. The power of support during my time of hardship is etched in my heart as unforgettable. Life is good in the *Life After*.

PICK UP THE PIECES...

- Time may not heal all wounds, but forgiveness begins the process
- When life catches up to you unexpectedly, expect the power of peace to show up
- For every ebb, there is a flow

In what situation, or where in life do you need to adapt to change?

See, I am doing a new thing!

(Isaiah 43:19)

Think of a time when you had to move on or move forward, even if it was difficult. What did you do to get over?

Cast all your anxiety on him because he cares.

(I Peter 5:7)

"Out of suffering have emerged the strongest souls; the most massive characters are seared with scars."

Kahlil Gilbran

CHAPTER FIVE

Overcoming You

Rhonda's Story...

My daughter overdosed on drugs only a few days prior to my telling this story. Her daughter, my granddaughter, called me into the room and cried, "I can't wake her up!" I knew something tragic had happen. It wasn't like my daughter to ignore any of us. I got up from where I was sitting in the living room and walked to her bedroom door. There she was, lying lifeless on the floor. My automatic response was to call on the Lord. My other daughter called an ambulance immediately.

The rescue squad rushed in and began resuscitation efforts instantly. It was not a good prognosis, but there was something deep in my soul that assured me she would be revived. I didn't understand it amid the chaos, but there were remnants of peace as I watched the rescuers pound on my daughter's chest and transfer breath into her limp body. After what seemed like hours, they carried my daughter's body out of the house on life support.

Once at the hospital, the real work to save her life began. There were so many doctors and medical professionals around her bed—I couldn't count the number to be honest. They were doing everything within their powers to bring a young woman back to life. After hours of attending to her, the team exited the room with the hope that she would open her eyes. Their hope was my hope and mine theirs.

It was a critical time to say the least. I prayed for days and nights and trusted that God would show up at a time when I needed him most.

That morning came 5 days later. I had been awake most of the night and don't quite remember when darkness turned to light. In the early morning hours, God restored life into my child's body. Just when it looked as if all hope was gone, He showed up. He showed up just like the confidence that rested in my spirit a few days prior. He, my Creator, is truly the living God.

I can't stress the importance of establishing a relationship with God. None of us know when life will take a turn for the worst. However, what we do know is that there is a Higher power. There is a Creator who sits high and looks low. If we have the faith just as small as a mustard seed, He will appear. As a matter of fact, He is always with us.

A prayerful life that recognizes Jesus as my best friend has become a part of my routine. No matter what happens in my life, I have become hyper God-conscience and know a few things for sure:

- God wants the best for us
- God is in charge

The Bible says heaven and earth may pass away, but the word of God shall live. It's not only about hearing His word; it's knowing that the Word has come to take us from where we are to where we need to go.

In my daughter's story, God graced her with continued life. While this is powerful, it is also important to recognize those moments when His will doesn't immediately appear to be in our favor. At almost the same time as my daughter's episode, another young man in my community suffered from an overdose. Sadly, he did not pull through. I prayed for clarification, meaning, and guidance. After all, they both experienced the same thing, so why did God leave one and take the other? Just as clear as day, the Holy Spirit said to me, "I've known him before." I was stunned. This was not the young man's first overdose; he was warned by experiencing a similar encounter before. The young man had heard God's wakeup call but ignored it.

Like the young man, many of us ignore the warnings. Some are given more chances, some not. The reality is, God is in control. It all circles back to personal experience and how we choose to respond to God's word. God gives us an opportunity every day that he wakes us up to know him for who he is.

Yes, my daughter was given a miraculous second chance. Now it's up to her to decide what she's going to do with that encounter. What will be her *Life After?*

PICK UP THE PIECES...

- All things work together for the good of those who love God
- Life is a Spiritual experience
- Stay woke for the enemy comes to kill, steal, and destroy

When was a time things/events didn't appear to be in your favor? How did you respond?

"I lie down and sleep; I waken again, for the Lord sustains me"

(Psalm 3:5)

When was a time you felt as if you had favor on your life? How did you respond?

> *The Lord will guide you always; he will satisfy your needs in a sun-scorched land and will strengthen your frame. You will be like a well-watered garden, like a spring whose waters never fail.*

(Isaiah 58:11)

"The most beautiful things in the world cannot be seen or even touched. They must be felt with the heart.

Helen Keller

CHAPTER SIX

The Beauty of Life

Sonia's Story...

I was traveling through the United States on my book tour when I received the call. My brother was ill, and I needed to get back home. I come from a very close-knit family in the Caribbean, so the instant I heard the news I jumped on a plane. So as I landed, I headed straight from the airport to the hospital. Hearing the diagnosis, everything on my agenda came to a screeching halt. There was no way I was not going to be available to stay beside my brother's bedside.

The two-month journey of being with my brother every day and every night taught me a level of patience I had never known. If you were to meet my kids and ask them to name one quality they would wish their mom be blessed more with, they would both say *patience*. I've never been a patient person. Sometimes people look at me wearing very long braids and say, "You must be a patient person because surely it took hours to get those braids done." No. I'm a disciplined person, not a patient person. There's a huge difference between the two. I knew God wanted to work on that part of me through the journey of my brother's illness.

I was awake early every morning to get my brother to doctor appointments and made sure he took his medication during the night. The entire day was dedicated to picking up the pieces with him. I hadn't dedicated that level of care for my own children. But, in the midst of this painful time, I also experienced a love that I had never experienced.

If you're like me, you probably tell family and friends that you love them. Sometimes it becomes such a routine that we don't give a lot of thought to the feeling. In many cases we make the statement as an afterthought. But what I went through with my brother was a display of genuine, unconditional love. As we held hands, the connection was different from others we had spent together in the past 42 years. The newfound connection grew stronger and stronger with each passing moment. We sang, laughed, and cried together. Nothing else mattered—those moments belonged to my brother. For every day the art of patience was nourished in my soul, my faith flourished even more. I've always had a solid grasp of faith, but this experience prompted an expansion tenfold.

When I first arrived to see my brother, I felt the spirit of death in the room. It was time to contact the family and get everyone together. However, I was adamant that anyone in the room who did not have faith, must exit. I didn't want anyone in the room who didn't believe my brother could have a second chance at life. Our family prayed for what seemed like hours. We recognized God's Spirit as life and life was sustained in my brother's lungs.

After two short months, the second chance came to an end. I would have loved time to stand still, but the hours he was given allowed him to find peace with God, with his family, and with everything he thought went wrong in his life. I look back on the journey of those months with a full heart and the acknowledgement that my brother's life had purpose.

Every day that I looked at my brother, I was reminded of my eternal soul. Realizing you've heard this before, but life is not about the cars we drive or how big of a house we own. It's what we do for other people that matters. Life is about our purpose, our mission. My prayer is for alignment with my God-given mission and purpose. Without alignment, it's impossible to move forward. God orchestrated that time for me to be with my brother. The Creator knew what I needed to open my ears and eyes to what he has for me. When I reflect on those two months, my passion for serving God is reinvigorated. Though I prayed and asked God to allow my brother to live, him. I knew, no matter the outcome, I would praise Him. Yet I still want to know why, and as clear as I am writing this story I heard the Lord say Sonia I had to take him.

More than ever before, I'm more appreciative of life. I value the people around me. I love deeper every day, and the strength of my faith is unparalleled. I will always be grateful for the time I had with my brother. I was into a *Life After* and have been molded into the better person I am today.

PICK UP THE PIECES...

- Pray hard, love harder
- The inner man is an anchor to the soul
- Success is measured by faithfulness

What is your life purpose?

*You will show me the way of life, granting me the joy of your
presence and the pleasure of living with you forever.*

(Psalm 16:11)

What is your life mission?

For God is working in you, giving you the desire and the power to do what pleases him.

(Philippians 2:13)

"Time is a cruel thief to rob us of our former selves. We lose as much to life as we do death."

Elizabeth Forsythe Hailey

CHAPTER SEVEN

Just a Matter of Time

Sharon's Story...

I was imprisoned for five years. It was a time filled with pain, anguish, and shame. I lost everything important to me, including my two young children.

My children's father was involved in drugs, and it tainted both our lives. Everything changed when I was caught with his drugs on me. He would have been a harsher prison sentence of life behind bars, so

I took the rap for the charge. I believed this was the best decision for our family. The children could stay with their father and I would do a short time locked up. At least the children would not be without both parents for a long period.

I took the fall so my children, two and three years old, could grow up free from the system. Seared in my memory is their little hands pressed against the glass at the holding cell. They were so innocent. I remember telling my children, "Mommy's going away for a while." They were too young to understand but I felt they needed an explanation for my absence. Shortly after, the children left United States for Panama with their father, who was living as a fugitive. My sentence was five to twenty-five years.

The first time I heard God's voice was in the holding cell. The arresting officers thought I was in shock. I heard their voices subconsciously, but at the forefront God was speaking to me. He said, "I had to bring you down this path. I had to let you experience a situation so distasteful that you will never be able to go back." My experience behind bars lived up to His word.

While incarcerated I was always fearful of going to the chapel. My brother is a pastor and I was afraid of running into him during prison ministry. You see, my family had no idea I was locked up. I had moved to Panama so my family was not in contact with me. They assumed I was in another country and doing well.

Anytime a church ministry came to our grounds, I could feel God calling me to the chapel. Time and time again I refused. In my mind, I was not worthy of the church. I was mentally and emotionally paralyzed.

After five long years, I was released from prison. The additional five years on probation which was excruciating, especially because there was an ongoing search for my children's father. I was always being watched and had to be mindful of where I went. There was a constant fear and anguish lurking in the corner. Life was not peaceful at all, though I was from behind bars. Naively, I thought release from prison would be the end of the story. Life was more difficult than I had imagined. I couldn't get a job or find a place to live. Again, I felt unworthy of anything good and began to shy away from a social life. The shame was more than I could bear. There was no one to confide in so my pain was sealed, trapped in my body. Even though the cell doors had been opened, I created walls to block out reality. I was still locked up.

The club scene became my escape. My cousin and I were on the scene night after night. Then, while getting dressed to head out on the town, something stopped me in my tracks. I still don't know how the TV channel was on a Christian station, but the pastor gave a message that seemed to be talking directly to me. I remember him staring in the screen, "You need to come. God is calling you to get your life together. Come." The pastor went on to explain that it didn't matter what I had done, God would save me. According to his word, I could be delivered and set free. I listened to that message and collapsed in the bed. The night seemed long and I cried throughout the night.

As powerful as that moment was, I fell right back into my pattern of clubbing. The next night I was back in dance hall. and ended up at the club the following night. I tried to ignore what I heard on TV the day before, but I felt something pulling me again. This time I was on the dance floor. I stood frozen in the middle of the floor with a drink in one hand and a cigarette in the other. It was if I was the only person in the room. The voice in my head was clear, "I want you in church tomorrow." Without another thought, I dropped everything and went home. something was happening to me and I was afraid.

Though I had a few bad experiences at church when first attending, my mother encouraged me to remain steadfast. Compelled in my Spirit to do so, I gave my life to Christ. And, finally, after several long years, I got my children back. There was a great deal of pain in the reunion because my children were now 18 and 19 and had experienced deep rejection. Though they were always in my heart, I had to deal with rejection myself. I'm still dealing with that today, though I know God can restore.

Today, I have peace and joy. I found happiness in *Life After*. My struggles taught me three valuable lessons that I'm compelled to share with the world. First and foremost, you must recognize yourself, while admitting the truth of your deeds. Second, you have to make peace with your circumstances. Third, and perhaps the most difficult, you must learn how to genuinely forgive yourself. Only then can *Life After* be experienced for the better in the present.

PICK UP THE PIECES...

- To recognize who others are, you must know who you are
- Only the things left in the dark can shame you
- Regardless of your circumstances, your identity is who you are

Think of a time when you've felt shame or embarrassed by your actions. How did this feeling keep you in bondage?

Do not grieve, for the joy of the Lord is your strength

(Nehemiah 8:10)

*Is there someone or something you need to
forgive yourself for?
For all have sinned and fall short of the
glory of God*

(Romans 3:23)

CHAPTER EIGHT

In God's Timing

Celeste's Story...

At the turn of the 21st century, my husband and I had settled into our marriage. Not soon after, the same question started to hurdle— "When are you going to have a baby? I was quite hesitant about the idea, but my husband was ready. He seemed to align with society's norm. My husband would remind me, "If you love me, you'll have my baby." In my spirit I wasn't ready to be a mom. But I felt the pressure of

"If we take care of
the moments,
the years will take
of themselves."

Maria Edgeworth

being a 28 year-young female who had been married for a number of years. Not only was my husband focused on having children, I felt as if other people were looking at me as if something was wrong with me.

With time I eased into the idea of motherhood. I was fully invested in our next family chapter and a few months after trying, we were pregnant. The news of our new addition to the family spread quickly. It's amazing how Western society celebrates this milestone. Pregnancy was great.

And then the unthinkable happened. At about 28 weeks I noticed heavy spotting and was taken to intensive care. It all seemed so sudden, but I progressed to preterm labor, then full labor. Everything happened so quickly, and no one knew why. It would be only after a few days and tests later that doctors identified harmful fibroid tumors were growing along with the baby.

I delivered the baby and he was taken out of the room. I could hear the nurses talking about surgery.

I wasn't sure what was happening, but I knew my son was alive. He was alive.

About 40 minutes later, the attending nurse came approach my bed and glared solemnly towards me. It was almost if she was looking through me but towards me at the same time. The movement of her lips reminded me of a scene from a movie happening in slow motion, "Your son did not make it." I was a complete wreck. A social worker and hospital chaplain were summoned to the room to counsel and console me. My cries were intense and overwhelming.

Eventually one of the nurses asked if I wanted to hold my son before he would be taken away again. Those moments were invaluable—I had a chance to cradle him in my arms, look at him, touch him, and count ten fingers and ten toes.

Sharing the news was almost unbearable. Everyone was in as much disbelief and I was. How could this have happened? I was drowned with feelings of sorrow and uncertainty. Celebrations that had been planned for months were suddenly canceled, leaving sadness and pity in their wake. People continued to call. Each time I recounted the events to someone, I was forced to relive the pain. The funeral offered some closure, but not much. It's hard to explain the feeling of losing a child—I didn't get an opportunity to see him grow, but I felt his potential. I knew him from the womb. This was a different grief than the loss of my dad or grandmother.

My husband and I were arguing nonstop. We blamed each other and pointed fingers every chance we could. I reminded him repeatedly, *I didn't want to do this in the beginning, and now look what happened.* That thought began to haunt me as people asked if I felt guilt. The suggestion was that perhaps I was to blame because I didn't want to get pregnant for so long. When I reflect, I felt anger more than anything else. Underneath the anger, embarrassment lingered. People tried to reassure me, "You're still a woman, even if you're not a mom." I never had those thoughts but realized that's what was going through everyone else's minds.

Six weeks later, I went back to the doctor for a checkup. She took routine tests to make sure I was healthy. When she reentered the room, I could tell that something wasn't right. My heart started to flutter – *my gosh what could be wrong now? Maybe the fibroid tumors were cancerous.* I looked up at her, "Celeste, you're pregnant." I was startled. A mixture of anxiety ignited throughout my entire body. It was a strange intersecting of emotions, but the memory of my son and the spirit of my future child brushed together in one space.

The doctors watched me carefully throughout the pregnancy. I was warned that the baby may have a brain bleed or need physical therapy, so I had to be ever so careful. Several months later I delivered a healthy brown bundle of joy, my daughter. She is a walking testament to the power of God's timing. Since the time she enrolled in school, our daughter has been a top student. Eighteen years later, she is on her way to college. Brain bleed, not my daughter.

Bad things happen to good people all the time. I've learned that we must push through the pain in order to become better and to reach a greater understanding of our situation. Through it all, I learned the importance of taking time with the Lord to sync with the spirit inside of me to reach my *Life After* every time.

PICK UP THE PIECES...

- Tension doesn't necessarily mean something is wrong…it means something is happening

- Dig deep— most of us are stronger and braver than anyone has ever taught us to believe

- The atmosphere you create is the one you get… create an atmosphere of hope

What current perspectives do you have that are driven by external circumstances or perspectives?

Do you see that faith was working together with his works,
and by works faith was made perfect?

(James 2:22)

Rest in the peace of God. What does He want you to settle into the peace of in this season?

Now the Lord of peace himself give you peace
always by all means.
The Lord with you all.

(2 Thessalonians 3:16)

"The first step towards getting somewhere is to decide you're not going to stay where you are."

J.P. Morgan

CHAPTER NINE

Starting Over

Lori's Story

I was in a same-sex relationship. My life was trapped for years in a situation that I knew was not right. When the madness finally came to a head, I was both delighted and broken. The breakup was God talking. I had spoken to God and made my request, "I wanted out of this and I don't know how to walk away." I didn't know how to do it in my own strength, I needed God's help. I was so concerned about everyone else's feelings; my convictions were going through the roof. That's when life as I had been experiencing started to disintegrate.

My finances were in shambles and I was an emotional and spiritual wreck. The decision to leave the relationship was the right thing to do, but it meant returning home at 38 years-old to live with my parents. So much time had been wasted and I wallowed in regret.

The Scripture reads in Isaiah 6.3, "To give unto them beauty for ashes." Though I was miserable, I believed that God was going to turn the ashes of my life into something good. Through this painful time, I learned that God will use the worst of situations to bring about something beautiful.

When I thought about starting over, there were so many pieces scattered about that I didn't know where to begin. How does one move forward when you feel you've done so much wrong? I was ashamed for allowing myself to get snatched by the sin of lesbianism. But I continued to believe that my future would somehow be better than my past.

I talk a lot about the word of God because that's the core part of my life. One of the things that helped me is a Scripture in 2 Chronicles 25. There was a king named Amaziah who was readying for battle. He had paid mercenaries scores of monies to fight on his behalf. A prophet came to him and said, "God does not want you to use those mercenaries. He's going to give you the victory of the battle through Him. Set them aside, let them go." King Amaziah didn't want to listen because he'd already spent all this money, however, he did as instructed. The lesson here is that God is able to give us much more than what we think we will forfeit if we follow what He wants for us. No matter how much you think you've lost or had to give up, God has more to give. The question becomes, what are you holding on to that you need to give up for the glory of God?

It's been many years since that breakup. I've gained a million times better than what I released. I can say with all certainty to any person who has been in any situation, whether it be an ungodly lifestyle or another personal struggle, there is restoration, recovery, and hope in your future. The transition is never easy when coming out of something where you've entangled your emotions or your money. However, the grace of God can lead you into greater. If you hold on to God and allow him to embrace you, you are guaranteed peace and success. I know what it's like to start over from a broken place and see God make you every bit whole. My life is not only a testimony, but an instrument to lead others out of the bondage of ungodly relationships. God can heal you from any addiction or give you the power to escape. His word tells me this is true. **My life is proof.**

There are better days. Don't quit!!!! My *life after* has become a catalyst of boundless love and favor.

PICK UP THE PIECES...

- Change is often uncomfortable, so is growth for a better you

- Freedom is a proclamation

- Let go of the good so you can experience the Awesome

Sometimes we go emotionally bankrupt while holding on to someone or some circumstance that is draining. What price are you willing to pay in your unwillingness to let go?

LORD, thou hast heard the desire of the humble:
thou wilt prepare their heart, thou wilt cause thine
ear to hear:

(Psalm 10:17)

For where your treasure is, there will your heart be also (Matthew 6:21). Where is your treasure? Where is your heart? The fruit you bear gives clues to both questions.

Ye shall know them by their fruits.
Do men gather grapes of thorns, or figs of thistles?
Even so every good tree bringeth forth good fruit;
but a corrupt tree bringeth forth evil fruit.

(Matthews 7:16 -17)

CHAPTER TEN

The True Me

Joysetta's Story...

For most of my life, I worked in careers that didn't excite me. As a matter of fact, I was generally stressed. *Life After* started after retirement.

Before retirement, my career started at the New York Telephone Company a long time ago. I'm 80 years old now, so there were a string of jobs after retirement and up to this time. I did manage to remain another

"We are constantly invited to be who we are."

Henry David Thoreau

job for 22 years as a staff director. However, I wasn't crazy about the work I was hired to do. Most of the time I was aggravated and often dealt with people who were aggressive in advancing their career. I'm not the type to compete for positioning so I settled in for the ride in the same position until I left that organization. Who knows if I would have stayed longer, but when management announced that flex-time would no longer be an option, I was done. I knew I did not want to work in an environment where my time would be controlled or monopolized.

Amid my newfound free time, I heard of a man by the name of Dr. Roots. Dr. Roots was a genealogy specialist. Interesting in the topic, I attended one of his lectures and was excited about what he shared. I was fascinated about genealogy and the course of my retirement was changed for the better. At the start, not many family or friends supported the idea of me working in the field of genealogy. Most thought the topic itself was crazy. Genealogy wasn't "in" back in the 1980's -- why would I ever want to do that?

Nevertheless, my husband encouraged me to pursue it. I come from a mixed heritage of Irish and African American, so he thought this was a cool idea.

One of the first things I did was to begin my own family roots. On the Irish side of my family, I found roots in the U.S. that traced back to 1840. I learned that my grandfather was denounced from his family and disinherited because he married my grandmother who was from a show business family. I didn't find much beyond my grandmother on her side of the family.

My husband's roots are in North Carolina. He spent a lot of time with his grandmother and she passed down stories about how his great-great-grandfather came out of slavery. His grandmother told him how his great-great grandfather purchased land. It was easy to keep track of the marriages and extended family because they owned the Hundred Acre Ridge. No one moved too far away. We were able to trace 400 relatives across of my husband's vast family tree. I was impressed and captivated by the entire process.

Inspired by the process of finding my husband's genealogy, we both decided to start a business, The African Atlantic Genealogical Society. As the business grew, we traveled to local schools and talked to students about the importance of genealogy and legacy. While at Medgar Evers College (Brooklyn), we noticed the class was very receptive but didn't ask any questions. They were sitting very quietly, seemingly disinterested. This was odd since we were normally bombarded with questions at these visits. When we asked the group for their feedback, one student said, "Well, most of us are from the Caribbean and you are talking about African Americans and Africa. Our ancestors would come from other places, too." This was an aha moment and lead us on another interesting quest.

We reflected on the student statement and realized we weren't using our full potential. We were the African Atlantic Genealogical Society because we could help trace anyone of African descent who had crossed the Atlantic Ocean— not just to the U.S.

That broadened our spectrum and pushed us to grow. Eventually this journey led me to the African American Museum of Nassau County. In the beginning we offered free services for anyone in the community to have their genealogy traced. Soon enough, we were given a dedicated genealogy room in the museum. There was a profound joy in helping people find their ancestors. It fills in a lot of blanks and allows people to feel like a real person with a history. Schools centrally focus on the experience of Africans as slaves. However, while slavery is a chapter, it is not the full story. In fact, there were thousands of Africans who came over from the continent and were not enslaved. They travelled here before this country was known as America. With these insights, we were able to connect several people with their ancestors and with immediate family members who are still living.

In my efforts to put my own puzzle together, I was helping others pick up their pieces along the way. Eventually I was asked to manage the county museum. This gave us the opportunity to dive